THIS

Somatic Compassionate

Grief

THIS

Somatic Compassionate

Grief

Tyona Y. McGee-Ezeilo

Book and Cover Art by Jordyn Ezeilo and Tyona Y. Ezeilo

ISBN 978-1-964776-00-2 Paperback format

ISBN 978-1-964776-01-9 ebook format

Publisher:
Envisionry Media

Envisionry Media
Creativity & Inspiration

Please direct book inquiries to:
Connect@Tyona-ME.com

To every
moment of
courageously
living with loss.

AN INTRODUCTION

I imagine upon entering the world we feel it, _all_.

> The sensation of the deliverer's touch. Temperature shifts from climates internal to external. Vibrations of unprecedented sound waves beating against our ear drums. The paradox of pressure 'release' and 'increase' from the crown of our skulls to the tips of our toes as we leave the container we were cooked within and begin to absorb the peace (or anxiety) of the auras sharing our 'new' world. Every inch of our skin receiving what the universe is transmitting in that moment we first arrive. We move with each breath, with these burgeoning **feelings**, creating sensory impressions of this unexplored existence.

Our unfamiliar emergence.

At some point, a **thought** is formed about this in-experienced _life_.

We may be directed (guided over time) to divide the two. Taught to form distinctions between the sensational emotion and the rational cognition; To prioritize one over another.

Do _you_ find it difficult to separate: the thinking and the feeling?

Does the mind respond with tethered connections to the body?

Does the body gently-spontaneously reflect ponderings of the mind?

Do tears _sting_ eyes and cloud vision when you -

Remember?

Do cheeks become flushed with warmth?

Does the nose begin to leak?

Do you try to find fast flight for excavating thoughts to land upon memories that reach -

not quite so deep?

We, at a time, were not trained to restructure reality, limit beliefs, or suppress natural emotional states.

I imagine that there was once a time, I only knew, how to _feel it, all_.

THIS Somatic Compassionate Grief

My Grief has historically, primarily, been pretending & ignoring.

Now, trying noticing & allowing.

THIS Somatic Compassionate Grief

All

feelings

thoughts

Life

sting

Feel It

All

THIS Somatic Compassionate Grief

My Somatic Compassionate Grief:

Listening more carefully
to my body's words to me.

Throat blocked.
Pursed lips.
Wells swell eyes.
Caved throat.
Mouth-trapped
Screams.

Lead-laden lids,
Heavy and sore.

Leaky lids

Inconveniently timed.

THIS Somatic Compassionate Grief

Old school hip hop.
Bass beats.
Heart-rhythms.

Reminders...

This Heart
once pulsed,
without
aches.

My Mother's Day of Birth.

Remembering her dance.

Her smile.

The expressiveness of her eyes.

Her friendships.

Her helpfulness.

Her cooking.

Her caring

For my son.

Her sewing.

Her typing.

Her cleaning.

Her organization.

Her creativity.

Her abilities.

The obstruction
of her abilities.

Today, I'm compelled to pretend & ignore.

THIS Somatic Compassionate Grief

Lost.

Back side to belly.

Shifting this side to the next side.

Then, to the first.

Restless sleep.

Awakening frequently.

Morning callings to greet my sheets,

as loud and pronounced as those in the *Eve*.

I catch myself,

Seemingly air

Flowing clumsily

Trapping loss

Lodging unwanted cries

In the center

Of my throat.

Walking.

Driving.

Talking

Through blocked passageways.

Navigating

Spaces

Both Familiar

And Unique.

I catch myself.

Remember,

...Breathe.

THIS Somatic Compassionate Grief

There is a sting in *good.*
"Good" feels deceptive.
The morning does not feel *good.*
The afternoon does not feel *good.*
Neither the evening nor, the night feels *good.*
This moment feels absent of pure goodness.
The term "good" in reference to my experiences of this day no longer
sits well with my soul.

This moment is here.
I am here in this moment.
I am breathing.
I am here.

Some moments moving,
Some moments still.

I am living.

I am breathing.

I do not feel *good.*

Who will sit alongside grief?

For days? Months? Years?

Who will allow themselves to see

-     unceasing tragedy -

in another's eyes?

                    Smile?

                              Movement?

Who will listen to loss, reliving repetitive recollections in places

where no new ones can be created?

Who can bear witness to pain personified in *every* conversation?

THIS Somatic Compassionate Grief

Why is it custom (*for some*) to motion through grief so rapidly, quietly and solitarily?
Who can endure the lengthy, loud, longing for the desperate miracle of returned life?

Laughter.

Mindlessness.

In This, my cheeks round,

My eyes squint,

My body shakes.

I hear a chuckle.

The sound emanated from me.

I laughed.

I realize, I've laughed.

Then, I remember.

The world is without you.

My body tenses.

THIS Somatic Compassionate Grief

I look around.

Maybe, you will visit me.

Maybe, again in my sleep.

Maybe, when I am awake

I will begin to see and hear you.

Maybe, have conversations with you,

Like in a mystical movie plot.

Maybe people will think my rational mind is blocked.

Maybe I will have learned to see

And hear beyond this reality.

Maybe you will visit me.

Maybe.

Like in the book we read as teens: Lois Duncan's, "Stranger with my

Face,"

Maybe

In those final moments you learned to make

Your loving sweet soul project astrally.

Maybe yours guided your dad's to accomplish the same feat.

Maybe you both

will visit me.

Maybe.

Because I can't imagine you being - not here.

I can't accept you being - no where?

You have to be -

somewhere.

Why not - here?

Maybe, again in my sleep.

Please.

Visit me.

THIS Somatic Compassionate Grief   15

I feel my heart breaking.

It is not just
This.

It is many
      mini
This'.

But THIS
is such a massive, THIS.
Not just an ache, a pain, a tear, piercing, fracture, break or a crack.
This broken part is beginning to crumble.
Shattered pieces, grinding into dust.

There is MORE
To
THIS.

THIS Somatic Compassionate Grief

Day 1 through Day 10
I kept feeling
a missing limb.
Wondering
is this what it feels like
to lose a twin?
Regretting all the time
and all the space.
All the days
I let waste.
Acknowledging, how in recent years
we walked the world
apart.
Today, unable to create words
for feeling such vividly
missing bodily parts.
Taking for granted
there would be moments
to reunite.
Time for planning
and preparation.
Looking forward to
reminiscing.
Thinking it could be later scheduled.
Thinking there was no need
to make haste.
Thinking our lives are so busy.
Forgetting
I don't control fate's
pace.

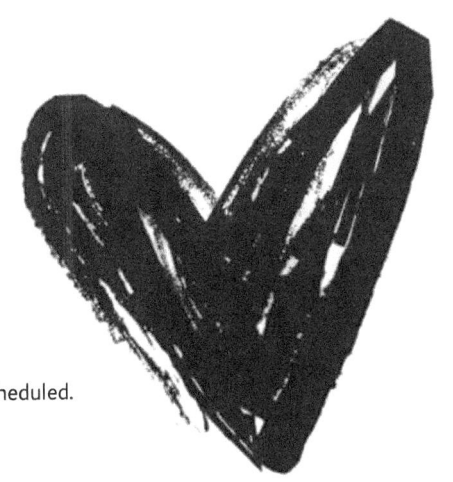

THIS Somatic Compassionate Grief

THIS Somatic Compassionate Grief

Motion
Pictures
Smiles
Candids
Familiar familial facial
Expressions.
At times, I crave images.
Other times, it's devastating
to engage in the action of
imagining.

THIS Somatic Compassionate Grief

No.

"I'm OK."

Let me rid any evidence otherwise

from my face.

"I'm not wallowing in sadness."

Let me engage in conversation

as my mind drifts

beyond your words.

"I'm listening."

Let me rest in my silence.

Let me nod, raise an eyebrow

match your emotions.

Although, I'm unclear the topic

of our current discussion.

"I'm OK."

Let me adjust my posture

to appear still capable

of holding myself up.

"I'm OK."

I have to be.

"I'm OK."

You can enter.

"I'm OK."

You can approach me.

"I'm OK."

You can release your fear of seeing me,

NOT ok.

THIS Somatic Compassionate Grief

Used exclamations
for the first time again
without feeling like I was
abandoning *something*.

Responding to news
of health improved.

Celebrating renewed
hope
in the existing possibility

of ***someone's***
recovery.

THIS Somatic Compassionate Grief

Distractions

THIS Somatic Compassionate Grief

Grieving with others
means, what?
How do you know when to do,
say, ask, share, cry, rage, conceal,
distract?
I want to inquire, 'Did, too, your heart
crack
randomly
wide open
uncontrollably, in public?'

Do you find yourself staring into
a screen?
Rewinding?
Rereading?
Traveling?
Not remembering
exactly where your mind has been?

What do you do
when your desire is
to crawl
into a ball?

When you're uncertain
You can take anymore?

THIS Somatic Compassionate Grief   25

Many weeks later
and, still,
a wakefulness in my slumber.
Still,
a dream state
as each day breaks.
Never fully awake
or, at rest.
This grief
is exponentially,
more complex.

THIS Somatic Compassionate Grief

Random pangs
and tightening.

Tension.

Back
Abs
Ribs
Chest
Heart

Trying to shift.

Locate places
that have escaped the pain.

There have to be places that
don't hurt.

Find them.

After encouraging my children to value the time they have with each other because we never know when the time will end, and sharing my commitment to be more intentional about spending time with our extended family, my 13-year-old daughter, gently, thoughtfully asked me, if you spend time getting closer to your family members, won't it just hurt more when they die?

Yes. It will.

When that time comes, prayerfully, they will have felt how much they mean to,
and are loved by me.

THIS Somatic Compassionate Grief

Not sure how I arrived here.

THIS Somatic Compassionate Grief

Death, the medal won in the marathon of life.

Death, the prize received for the gift of life.

Where are you now?

THIS Somatic Compassionate Grief

What was I doing?

I close my eyes.
I see their smiles.
I hear their laughs.
I feel their hugs.
I open them,
and remember.
There is something
that feels
seemingly
unmanageable
about remembering,

In the dark.

THIS Somatic Compassionate Grief

I don't know what I was looking for?

THIS Somatic Compassionate Grief

Grief Circle
Tonight.

I prayed.
I created space.
I listened to loss.
I reflected on lessons and blessings.
I sought wisdom.
I felt the fear and confusion.
I acknowledged the
impermanence of relationships.
I celebrated time.
I shared regrets.
I celebrated life.
Tonight,
we paused
and breathed -

Together.

THIS Somatic Compassionate Grief

It hurts. A lot. Often. I want to say it will pass. The reality of my experiences is that it doesn't. I just ignore it's presence. There is so much I cannot bring myself to say aloud, yet.

Love you deeply. Xo

Searching for peace in pain.

"Wishing everyone moments of unexpected joy and peace this week."

THIS Somatic Compassionate Grief

How am I going to finish uploading these?

Memories.

Acknowledging,
I cannot be alone
with this.

THIS Somatic Compassionate Grief

God,

Thank You for the wisdom, strength, concern and compassion
of these people.

I have needed these people:

JTP. JB. JEE. JDYM. YM. TM., TE. CW. PM. TKDE, JMGE, TJE, JAKE.
JM. DM, CLS, KM. CM. SF. TC. JE. KH. TC. CJ. AJ. KS. DD. MK. AWG.
BE. BEC.

I pray they know their significance to me.
Please help me to show up for them throughout their lives
in meaningful ways.

Perspective matters.
When people can look
through a kaleidoscope
of lenses
And see with clarity their own story
while also glimpsing
and choosing to sharpen
their Focus
on the various narratives
of others:
There is a grace.
There is a gentleness.
There is a presence
that soothes.
That says,
Here is me.
I feel...
I think...
I believe...
I am here.
And asks,
Where are you?
Acknowledging
I see you...
I hear you...
I am with you...
Reflecting
Another's story
Without confusing it
With their own.

THIS Somatic Compassionate Grief

I've had to learn and practice

this shift.

Awkwardly.

Over time.

I am

beyond grateful

I am not alone

Because

I need

People like you

Surrounding me.

Those who

intentionally

Choose

to

Create space

for exploration.

THIS Somatic Compassionate Grief

43

Ways I push

It farther

from my mind:

Head shakes.

Blinks.

Refusals- "No!"

Denial- "That couldn't have happened!"

Fantasy- "Maybe this is an alternate universe."

THIS Somatic Compassionate Grief

Quick, sudden pinches
At my heart.

THIS Somatic Compassionate Grief

How many emotions can be experienced by one person in a single day?

I grew up with such a huge family. I believe God knew my spirit
needed all those converging energies to wrap around me and carry me
through my childhood & younger adult life.

You don't know, unless you know.
If you know me, you know.

Breathe with me. Pray with me. Rage with me.
Scream with me. Grieve with me.
Rejoice with me. Celebrate with me.

Pray for me and everyone who may be feeling
such intensely powerful emotions
right now.

THIS Somatic Compassionate Grief

Needing all your legs to help hold me up, as I run to catch up with the current pace of change (because at the moment, my two don't seem to be enough).

THIS Somatic Compassionate Grief

I keep losing my place.

Forgetting my thoughts.

Yesterday, - I'm having a hard time remembering yesterday.

Today, - remembering my process and my purpose.

And, if I'd eaten today?

I did.

Once.

I remembered to take a vitamin.

Not all,

But one.

Bouncing from phone to tablet -

I keep forgetting,

What am

I searching for?

His unraveling

around revisiting grief

Met with

my physiological need

for quiet solitude

increasing -

And mental patience thinning -

Are all conspiring,

loosening my lips

...and multiplying

my use of expletives.

THIS Somatic Compassionate Grief

THIS Somatic Compassionate Grief

Aren't you sad?

Like, *ALL* the time?

THIS Somatic Compassionate Grief

It's Sadness
Grief
Guilt
Regret.

It's Shock
Disbelief.

It's fear.

THIS Somatic Compassionate Grief

There is a space.

A void.

A depth of emptiness

that I can sometimes reroute my consciousness from:

Only breath

flows there.

THIS Somatic Compassionate Grief

We are not granted enough time

To be lost

And find ourselves again.

THIS Somatic Compassionate Grief

The weight of my body.

Heavy, dense, immobilized.

Light, frail, floating.

Invisible

To them.

I'm simply,

Here.

Am I?

THIS Somatic Compassionate Grief

There is a fire that ignites
the caves of my nostrils
before a sting rounds
the balls of my eyes -
And a thick rock, blocks
my airway
Lodging, awkwardly,
Just beneath my chin.
Within seconds,
I feel its flame.

The moisture
enveloping each eyelid
with every blink.
Each nostril,
with every breath.

Sniff.
Wipe.
Breathe.
Sniff.

THIS Somatic Compassionate Grief 59

When I can keep my awareness above the ache in my heart,

It doesn't seem to break open.

THIS Somatic Compassionate Grief

You've decided to what?

Grief isn't logical.

That helps and doesn't harm?
Do that.

We will *never* be here as we were.

I feel that truth's constriction in my fingers, neck, back and eyes.

THIS Somatic Compassionate Grief

Random soreness

Upper arms

Lower legs

Muscle spasms

Shooting nerve pain

THIS Somatic Compassionate Grief

THIS Somatic Compassionate Grief

I recognize the strength it takes
to be in pain and rise, move,
And push through.

I applaud those who
are crumbling -
And still standing upright.

I'm just going to lay here
Right now,
and whisper, 'I love you'
to the numerous parts of *me* that
are hurting -
And **s c r e a m i n g**
for

Recognition.

THIS Somatic Compassionate Grief

THIS Somatic Compassionate Grief

There is a yearning to be everywhere:
Close to the seasoned
who continue involuntarily shedding
pieces of themselves.
Beside the novice
whose first layer of flesh
has been torn from its home.
Aside the youth, witnessing
the undefined.
Holding the hopeless,
the collapsed,
the confused.
In the company of the busied,
the deniers,
the soft-spoken
struggling.
Near the angry,
the howlers,
the trembling,
the faithful,
the hope-searchers.

Carefully listening to
the silence-stricken.

There is a yearning to be absolutely everywhere:
With those hunting, gathering,
grasping,
reconfiguring -
The pieces left behind
And the pieces - taken with you.

THIS Somatic Compassionate Grief   67

THIS Somatic Compassionate Grief

How?

The world is continuing to spin.

Weddings and Vacations

Holiday celebrations and births

Joy still exists somewhere

Here

They lost their angelic mother

and they embrace life

with the spirit of saints.

They lost a cherished child

and they advocate with loving passion

for the children of the world.

They lost treasured spouses

And they still see beauty in the coming day.

They lost grandparents, and parents, aunts, uncles, siblings,

children, colleagues, neighbors, best friends

And their worlds continue to spin.

Please order my steps Dear Lord,

to allow my inner world to one day hold space for -

and spin with the pure joy

I imagine -

surrounding me.

THIS Somatic Compassionate Grief

THIS Somatic Compassionate Grief

Deep sighs

And head shakes

How can any of this possibly

Be

Real?

THIS Somatic Compassionate Grief   71

Rambling
And
Rambling

THIS Somatic Compassionate Grief

Temporal twinges.

Each statement feels
Insensitive
And
Offensive

Unconscious Declarations
Of Privilege.

When mourning,
Presentations of *Haves*
Magnifying
What We
Now
Have not.

I am choosing

To rest

Firmly

On my back

Cradling my knees

Feeling the curve

In my spine

The lift

Of my bottom

Rocking my pelvis

Side to side

Allowing the stretch of my hips

Pointing and flexing

my wiggling toes

Rubbing my thighs against my bare belly

Breathing to the pace

Of the brushing strokes

Of cool air

From the a/c

Planting light kisses along my arms

Elbows to shoulders

Lengthening my neck

And raising

My head.

Noticing

My dry eyes.

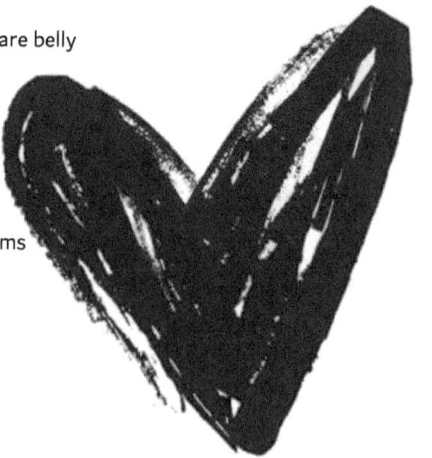

THIS Somatic Compassionate Grief

We are temporary.

Again,

So much I can not bring

Myself

To

Say

THIS Somatic Compassionate Grief

THIS Somatic Compassionate Grief

'Thinking of you'

Isn't strong enough

As I transition

Through my day

I wonder

How you've slept?

Are you awake?

Is it too early to call?

What if you're just finding a way to close your eyes

Are you eating?

Have you returned to work?

How's your health ?

Are you eating healthy?

Are you seeing your doctors?

Are you sharing your feelings with a therapist?

Are you surrounded by friends?

Are you feeling lonely?

Are you staying busy?

Are you overwhelmed?

Do you feel safe?

Do you have everything you need?

How can I help?

Are you showing yourself love?

Is it too late to call?

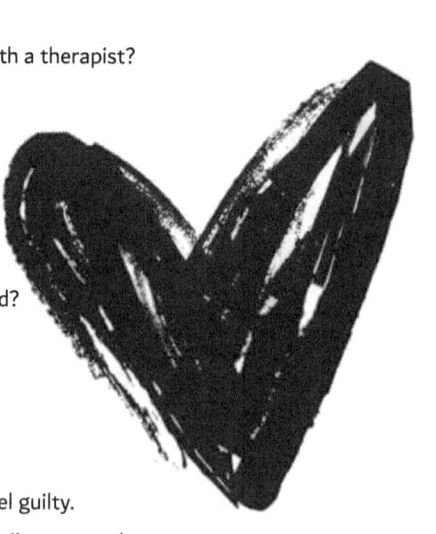

When I don't reach out daily I feel guilty.

When I do reach out I worry that I'm too much.

Am I triggering feelings of depression?

Am I glazing over your desire to vent?

Is the focus of our conversations too peppy?

THIS Somatic Compassionate Grief

Am I totally annoying?

Do I tell you, I can't stop crying?
Do I keep asking, how are you?
How do I find ways to express my love, and sadness?
Do I tell you how much I worry about you?

There's so much peeking from behind, 'I'm thinking about you.'

I'm tired.

THIS Somatic Compassionate Grief

But, they are two of my favorite voices.

How?

THIS Somatic Compassionate Grief

When my vision blurs

Like a movie fade out

And I can't recall the topic of my last

Thought

I should head

To bed

Yesterday, I felt fine.

Today, It's back.

THIS Somatic Compassionate Grief

Bizarre

Weeks later,

Raising the lids of my eyes at 6am

To the natural alerts of nature

Hearing birdsong

And rooster crow

As the sound of my inner voice

Forms the first thought of this day,

"Flash flooding"

THIS Somatic Compassionate Grief

Ouch!

Nervous bolts

Weakening mobility

From wrists to fingertips.

Aching arms

Beginning

below

each elbow.

Rods and pins

Vibrating

Throughout my

upper limbs.

Relentless,

Reverberating,

Pain-quakes.

THIS Somatic Compassionate Grief

Vacillating

Between forgetting to eat

And

Forgetting I've eaten already

THIS Somatic Compassionate Grief

Hunger pangs

Focusing on what doesn't hurt.

THIS Somatic Compassionate Grief

There's an opening and a closing.

Is my Acceptance a derivative
of Denial?
Acknowledging the
Physical pain
And
Emotional strain
of Anger & Depression.
Acknowledging the
Futility
of Bargaining
in my rejection
of Meaning.
Feels like I am bordering
the parts of myself
that require
the greatest *Healing.*

Staging.

THIS Somatic Compassionate Grief

Comprising a "Requests for memorial service information" list

Breaths shortening

THIS Somatic Compassionate Grief

When I stop...

watching TV, strolling the internet, eating, chewing, drinking, cleaning,

cooking, reading, listening to music,

talking.

When I'm still and quiet,

my breathing is irregular, my throat is thick, my chest is tightened, my

limbs are jittery, my mind is traveling,

yet present in what is, right now.

You are not here.

THIS Somatic Compassionate Grief

We don't talk or teach about death?

Our silence provides protection.
And pain.

"I Don't Know What to Say."

This.
This unknowable unknowing.
This is what kept me fleeing the work of grief.

In the space of spoken words, I've threaded together written ones.

I do not *know* what to *say*.

This.

This is what I am feeling.
Felt.
May someday, feel again.

Not speaking.
Not knowing.
Just feeling.

I am gently exploring how to remain
in this unknowable,
often unspeakable place,
 just long enough
to no longer fear it.

THIS Somatic Compassionate Grief

Take good care of yourself.

THIS Somatic Compassionate Grief

About the Author

In addition to her various job titles, Tyona is a daughter, sister, mother, wife, niece, cousin, and friend. Born and raised in the northeastern United States, her life journey has been influenced by her diverse roles and passions. She studied nursing, social work and psychology, each discipline contributing to her holistic understanding

 of human behavior and well-being. For the past 20 years, Tyona has worked as an independent consultant offering educational and support group services to both parents and professionals.

In her leisure time, she finds solace and rejuvenation through travel, and practices like yoga and Pilates, fostering a balance between physical and mental well-being.

A voracious reader and poet, she finds inspiration in words, both written and spoken.

While Tyona's roots lie in the dynamic, bustling, season-rich states of the northeastern USA, she currently calls the sunny landscapes of south Florida her home. Through her work with the coaching and consulting organizations she founded, Tyona continues her journey of growth, learning, and service to others.

THIS Somatic Compassionate Grief

Traveling leaves you speechless, then turns you into a storyteller.

– African Proverb

THIS Somatic Compassionate Grief

THIS Somatic Compassionate Grief